MOUNTAIN BIKING

THIRD EDITION

MICHAEL STRASSMAN

FALCON®

GUILFORD, CONNECTICUT
HELENA, MONTANA

AN IMPRINT OF THE GLOBE PEQUOT PRESS

A FALCON GUIDE ®

To Judy Strassman and Steve York, who helped write the chapters on maintenance and showed me their secret rides along the Salmon River.

Text and layout design by Casey Shain
Illustrations by Diane Blasius

ISBN 0-7627-2689-X
ISSN 1541-8537

Manufactured in the United States of America
Third Edition/First Printing

Contents

The Mountain Bike

Yesterday I rode my bike up a mountain. It did not take a lot of effort. I was gone for only a couple of hours. An easy trail, it gently rises up an ancient glacial moraine. Lanky pines shade the way past granite boulders and aspen trees. As I pedaled, I marveled at this machine, this tool.

The mountain bike combines the stalwart engineering of the motorcycle with the refined craftsmanship of the racing bike. It is one of the most efficient self-propelled instruments ever invented.

The surface of the trail is compact dirt. My wide tires bite firmly. By summer's end, this trail will be soft from hooves and boots—a mountain biker's nightmare. I will shift to my lowest gears and plow through it. For now, my effort is easy and rhythmic. I have become part of this forest.

The wildlands can present their own surprises. Boulders—remnants of a recent avalanche—have fallen across the trail. Their sharp corners could puncture a tire or flatten a rim. Confidently, I pull my front wheel up on them and pedal hard, slamming my rear tire against the rock. The wheel rises over the obstacle, grabs the firm soil, and propels me onward.

Should I get into trouble, I must rely upon myself. I carry all tools, all knowledge. A broken chain can be repaired, preventing a long walk out. A sudden storm will not make my ride uncomfortable. Even now, I cross a thin layer of snow, vestige of a recent tempest. My bicycle handles expertly through this new medium.

Finally, cresting the moraine, I enter a fairyland of white-rimmed pines. I slip on the snow, regain my straight line, and pedal toward the lake. The clouds have broken to reveal banners of gold light falling on frosted mountains. I pause at the scene, lower my seat, and descend.

The mountain bike has brought me to many wonderful places—places to which I never could have gone on my road bike. The skinny tires of my road bike would not grip the trail, the thin rims would crumble on the rocks. Mountain bikes give you the freedom to ride almost anywhere in any conditions. Your mountain bike can take you through snow, across streams, down old railroad grades, and into the backcountry. They are perfect for negotiating the rough terrain of the city. The mountain bike opens up a whole new world.

The majority of bicycles purchased today are mountain bikes. Their versatility and comfort have made them popular. When you first look at a mountain bike, you will notice several differences from your standard ten-speeds. The tires are the most obvious. Wide and knobby, these fat monsters provide better traction, shock absorption, and stability. They are more resistant to puncture and far more durable than skinny tires. So, mountain bikes are often called "fat-tire bikes" when compared to their delicate skinny-tire cousins.

Many recreational cyclists complain about the hunched-over, wind-resistant posture of racing bikes. On the mountain bike, you sit upright. Unlike the drop-style handlebars of racing bikes, the wide handlebars are designed for maneuverability and handling. All your controls are mounted here; the brakes are close to the hand grips, next to them are the shift levers. Stopping, shifting, and steering are all within fingers' reach.

Mountain bikes provide a wide range of gearing to make riding over varied terrain easier. Generally, mountain bikes are geared lower than road bikes. Most have anywhere from fifteen to twenty-seven speeds: five to nine sprockets on the rear and three chain rings on the front. The smallest chain ring is for ascending, the middle chain ring is for the flats, and the large chain ring is for descents. Mix and match them as you please!

The brakes are perhaps the most important component of any bicycle. The mountain bike's brakes are designed for durability and function in wet and muddy conditions. Get to know the brakes and how they work. An unsafe brake is an unsafe bike.

The heart of the bike is the frame. At first glance, a basic mountain-bike frame does not appear to be any different from other bikes. However, the uses and abuses of the mountain bike demand a sturdy but lightweight construction. Some mountain bikes use chrome-moly or aluminum. Others stray from the traditional double-diamond design. These high-tech bikes are constructed from Kevlar, carbon fiber, titanium, even magnesium with thermoplastic skins. Some are shaped like the letter Y and have both front and rear suspension. But whether the frame is traditional or futuristic, mountain bikes harbor some common design elements. Frames tend to have compact geometries for better handling, greater clearance for obstacles, and a lightweight but strong composition for durability and efficiency.

Most important, mountain bikes are designed for fun. Ride any-where, on all terrain, in any conditions. Relax in stability and com-fort, or push yourself up a steep hill. Remember, these machines take skill to operate and demand self-sufficiency on the part of the rider. An accident or breakdown could happen far from any help. But by knowing how your bike works, you avoid breakdowns; by concen-trating on developing your riding skills, you avoid accidents. Let's learn how it's done. Build your confidence and have more fun.

Choosing a Mountain Bike

When choosing a mountain bike, there are several things that should be considered. Decide what the primary use of your bike will be. Commuting? Racing? Fitness riding? Maybe it's just for play. Consider the terrain. Maybe backcountry trails? Or just down to the store for a dozen eggs? Price is another consideration. What are you willing to spend in exchange for quality and function? These questions must be asked before you walk into a bike shop.

Price

Quality mountain bikes range in price from $250 for an around-town bike to $7,000 for a custom-made, exotic-metal, dual-suspension racing bike. Lower prices mean a less durable, more basic mountain bike. Midrange bikes ($350 to $600) are the best value for the money. These are sturdy bikes that hold up to abuse but won't abuse your wallet. Higher priced bikes, which can run as high as $7,000, are designed for the serious enthusiasts and racers. These have exotic frame materials and highly refined component designs. They offer the best performance of any mountain bike.

After considering your budget, decide upon the intended use of the mountain bike. There are many different types of mountain bikes for a variety of needs. There are cruisers, hybrids, racing bikes, BMX bikes, and trials bikes. All of these can be used in the dirt, yet some are better for different applications.

Cruisers

For short commutes or light recreational riding, there's no need for a wide range of gearing or off-road equipment such as heavy suspension. Instead, consider an around-town bike. Gaining in popularity is the "beach cruiser" (Figure 1). This is a midweight bike with upright handlebars, one to five speeds, and a very comfortable, relaxed ride. These bikes resemble the old Schwinn cruiser frame: coaster brakes, fat whitewall tires, and a basket on the front.

Figure 1

Cruiser

Hybrids

If you expect to do your around-town riding quickly and efficiently, you may want a lightweight, multispeed, hybrid mountain bike or simply a "hybrid" (Figure 2). These bikes combine the efficiency of a road bike with the handling of a mountain bike. Designed with a geometry similar to road bikes, hybrids share many of the same components as true mountain bikes. Tires are fatter than a road bike yet thinner than a true mountain bike. The tires also have more tread

Figure 2

Hybrid

than a road bike, but smaller knobbies than a mountain bike. There is
a wide range of gearing. Many have rapid-fire thumb shifters, while
others have grip shifters. Most don't come equipped with shocks,
but some do have suspension seats, which help cushion the ride.
The hybrid is an excellent choice for city dwellers who have to
dodge such rim-bending obstacles as curbs and potholes. It is also a
good choice for rural cyclists who ride predominantly dirt and gravel
roads. The components and construction, however, are not designed
for extensive trail riding.

The Traditional Mountain Bike

This is the kind of bike most people think of when they hear the
words "mountain bike" (Figure 3). Designed to be used on rough
roads, backcountry trails, and/or challenging terrain, mountain bikes
fall into several categories. There are recreational mountain bikes, racing bikes, specialized mountain bikes, and mountain touring bikes.

Figure 3

The traditional mountain bike with front suspension

Recreational mountain bikes are designed for riding on dirt roads, through streams, over rock, and along trails. One of the more popular styles today, recreational mountain bikes provide a comfortable, stable ride in a variety of riding situations. With eighteen to twenty-seven speeds at your finger tips, these bikes are versatile in any terrain. A longer frame geometry combined with stability in steering makes it a more predictable riding bike.

Many traditional mountain bikes have front suspension or shocks. These absorb the bumps and can smooth out rough terrain. Shocks are heavier than traditional forks, but the trade-off is worth it, especially if you plan to ride backcountry trails.

Racing Mountain Bikes

Racing mountain bikes are designed for durability, efficiency, and high-speed maneuverability. Frames are constructed of ultralight-weight alloy steel, aluminum, titanium, Kevlar, or carbon fiber. A tighter frame geometry places your weight farther back over the rear wheel to increase traction on hills. A steeper head tube angle provides quicker, more precise handling. Componentry is built to perform smoothly in the worst environments and the most demanding situations. Manufacturers continue to improve components, making all parts lighter, stronger, and faster. Because racing bikes are on the cutting edge of mountain-bike technology, what you see on a racing bike today may become standard equipment for your recreational bike tomorrow.

Trials Bikes

Trials bikes (Figure 4) are another type of competitive bike that are designed to be jumped, hopped, and maneuvered over obstacles such as cars, logs, picnic tables, ramps, and boulders. The goal of trials is to perform these feats without your feet touching the ground (dabbing). Originally an event designed for motorcycles, trials have become a fascinating spectator sport for mountain-bike competition. Trials bike frames tend to be smaller than the standard mountain-bike design. They are also stiffer—reinforced to avoid frame flexing—which

Figure 4

Trials bike

enhances maneuverability. The tires have very little air pressure for maximum traction.

The Mountain Touring Bike

Similar to the recreational mountain bike is the mountain touring bike (Figure 5). Although designed for carrying loads in the backcountry, this bike is often seen touring on the road with skinnier tires. While the touring bike will take you anywhere that recreational bikes will, it has a more relaxed frame geometry (longer frame angles) suited for carrying loads such as touring gear. On the frame are three sets of studs for water bottle cages. Mounted on the front and rear are racks (panniers) for carrying gear. The gearing and componentry of this bike are similar to that on a recreational bike.

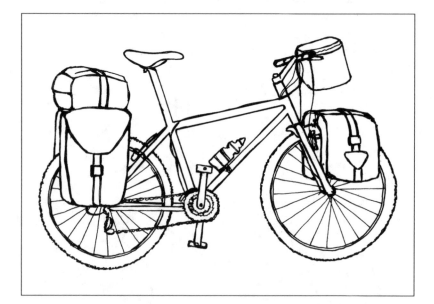

Figure 5

A mountain touring bike loaded down

BMX Bikes

Bicycle Motocross (BMX) bikes are those little trick bikes you see the neighborhood kids showing off with all the time. But don't shrug

Figure 6

A BMX bike

these cycles off as toys. There are six-year-olds that can outperform their big brothers on any vacant lot. BMX bikes were the first popular bikes to be ridden in the dirt. The latest rage is the freestyle BMX bike. Outfitted with features like frame stands, axle pegs, and slick tires, these bikes allow riders to perform gymnastic feats never imagined on a bicycle when the sport first emerged.

Hard-Tail vs. Full-Suspension Bikes

Full-suspension bikes (Figure 8) definitely look like the mountain bike of the future. Some of these bikes are shaped like the letter Y or are molded from a single magnesium spine with thermoplastic skins. The upside is that these bikes offer a smooth ride over even the roughest terrain. The front suspension absorbs bumps that would rattle your arms, while the rear suspension cushions, well . . . your rear. All of this innovation, however, does not come cheaply. Ask yourself, "How much do I want to spend?" and "Do I really need a high-tech, full-suspension, exotic metal bicycle with more gadgets than the space shuttle?" If the answer is yes to both questions—then go for it!

A good compromise is a traditional mountain bike with front suspension, typically called a "hard-tail" (Figure 7). A front shock absorbs many bumps but doesn't bounce around as much as its full-suspension cousin. Granted, it doesn't have the "techno" look, but since it has fewer moving parts, the hard-tail is lower maintenance.

The best bike for you is a matter of personal preference. Just don't limit yourself by buying a bike that is specific to one aspect of mountain biking. The joys of mountain biking come from a variety of experiences, be it racing, touring, or recreational riding. Ask around. Especially glean the advice of your bike shop; they will be up-to-date on the latest advances. Whatever you decide, be sure that you buy a bike that's comfortable and fun to ride.

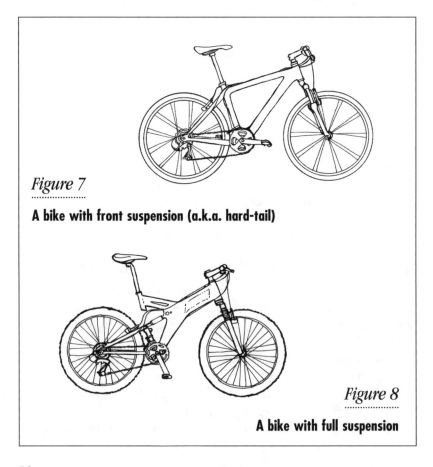

Figure 7

A bike with front suspension (a.k.a. hard-tail)

Figure 8

A bike with full suspension

Riding Skills

We all know how to ride a bike. The mountain bike is not any different until we get into the dirt. But before we go racing down any Kamikaze! downhills, let's learn a few of the basics on the flats.

Weight Shifts

Mountain bikes are remarkably stable. It doesn't take much effort to turn them. You'll notice that you can turn a mountain bike simply by shifting your weight and leaning slightly into the turn. This is important. Use your weight shift to initiate and hold turns. Use the handlebars for more precise movements. In a large sweeping turn, you can actually move the bike in the opposite direction of the turn while at the same time holding the bike in a lean. This quality enables the rider to steer around small obstacles in a high-speed curve. It is the increased stability from wide tires and suspension that allows you to do this.

Forward and rear weight shifts are important elements in mountain biking. There will be times when you will want to put more traction on the rear tire, or push your weight forward to clear an obstacle. Take the bike to an area of slippery traction and try standing up off the seat and pedaling. The rear tire will spin out in the dirt. Now sit on the seat and watch how much more traction you get. On road bikes, we are used to standing up in the saddle in order to give the bike more power. But on mountain bikes, especially on hills, it is important to sit down. This requirement tends to work different muscles than a road bike does. It pumps your quads instead of your calves.

Braking

Stopping the bike safely is important (Figures 9 and 10). Always pull on the rear brake before pulling on the front. Pulling on the front brake will quickly send you right over the handlebars. Try easing in on the rear brake and then squeezing the front brake tight as you stop. If you're braking while riding downhill, slide back in the saddle to put more weight over your rear tire.

Get to know what it takes to slow your bike down. Try coming to a dead stop at different speeds. When you get out in the woods, this knowledge will save you from an ugly collision with a rock or a log. It will also allow you to negotiate obstacles better. A lot of off-road skills combine speed with ability. Knowing how to slow your bike down to that perfect speed will help you out.

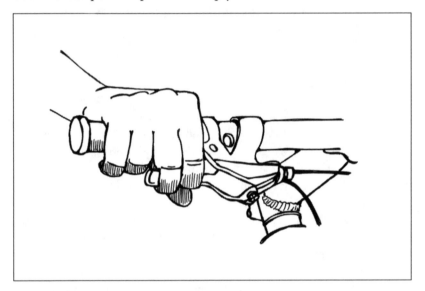

Figure 9

Proper braking grip

Turning

When going into a turn, slow down before the turn. There is nothing more frightening than realizing that you have entered a turn too fast. Turns often contain loose dirt and debris that can make the bike

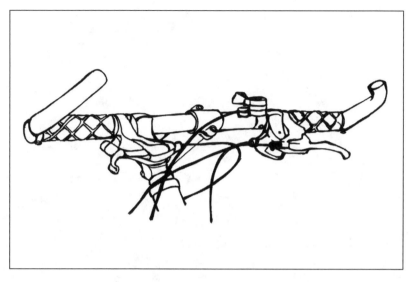

Figure 10

Braking system and gear shifters

really squirrelly as you decelerate. Pulling hard on the rear brake will skid out the rear tire, and pulling hard on both brakes might send you over the handlebars. Keep your speed down as you enter a turn. Lean around the turn smoothly, avoiding obstacles. If you are going too fast, try to keep the bike in a straight line as you bring the bike to a halt. Don't try to blast through the turn, hoping that you'll make it. Stop. It'll save you from a meal of dirt—or worse.

Skidding

Take the bike out into the dirt and practice skidding the rear wheel. Knowing how your bike responds in a skid may save you from a nasty fall. Start out slowly. Yank on the rear brake and throw your weight into the opposite direction of the turn, coming to a stop each time. Balance slightly with your inside foot, resting on it when you stop.

Once you've got the hang of it, instead of coming to a stop, try skidding and pedaling. (Perfect this technique until it becomes one smooth motion.) This is the skid turn, and it will really help you on curvy

Figure 11

Skid turn

descents, especially in soft sand (Figure 11). Use this method only as a last resort. Excessive braking and skid turns increase erosion and damage trails.

Skidding into a turn with one foot straight out touching the ground may be done on motorcycles, but it is considered bad form on mountain bikes. Style-wise, expert riders feel that a person should be able to control the mountain bike through proper lean and braking. The foot becomes a crutch, ready to help you out as you become off-balance. From a safety standpoint, that dangling foot could become caught on a branch or a rock and yank you off the bike, or worse, yank your foot into a sprain. However, in slow-speed maneuvering, a quick dab with the foot is OK. It can save you from falling over.

Balance

Have you ever tried to balance a bicycle while it was standing still? Velodrome riders call this a track stand. This is a very difficult technique to master, but it is definitely worth practicing. Often you will have to balance the bike while traveling at slow speeds. Areas of slippery traction, steep sandy uphills, and intricate obstacles all require keen balance and handling. Although some expert trials riders seem to be able to balance their bikes endlessly without movement, a little movement will be required for you to try it.

Cruise at a slow speed and use both brakes to bring you to a snail's pace. Loosen the straps on your pedals or unclip from your clipless pedals. Move your feet around on your pedals to maintain your balance. Now, as you lose momentum and start to feel out of balance, give a little power to the pedals, and brake. If you feel as if you are going to fall over, turn the front wheel in the direction you feel off-balance. It will keep you upright. Do it again. Practice will reduce wheel, foot, and leg movements until you can hold your bike at a standstill. You can now creep along far slower than you could ever pedal, while still keeping in balance.

Now work on expanding the idea. Put some rocks out in a tight slalom course in front of the bike. Now creep up and try maneuvering around them without falling over. After a while you will get quite proficient at slow-speed maneuvering.

As the conditions become more technical, you will want to add a wheelie or actual hopping into your slow-speed maneuvering. The wheelie (pulling the front wheel into the air) will help you shift the balance point (instead of simply turning the handlebars) as the front wheel comes down on the unbalanced side. Don't pull the wheel up really high; just pull slightly as you feel the bike begin to slow. This technique is especially important in sandy terrain.

Hopping

Hopping is a technique used by trials riders. It involves bringing your bike to a stop and bringing both wheels off the ground almost simultaneously (Figure 12).

It is done by clinching the brakes, bringing the bike to a stop, and pulling the front wheel up in a wheelie. At the exact moment the front wheel has reached its zenith, the back brake is released and power is applied while abruptly pushing your weight forward. The

Figure 12

Hopping over a boulder

rear tire leaves the ground and the bike is momentarily airborne.

Hopping is difficult to master on a conventional mountain bike and is more suited for BMX and trials bikes. However, variations on the theme will help you in rocky terrain. A more detailed explanation will follow in the obstacles section.

Gearing

Mountain bikes usually have eighteen to twenty-seven gears to work with. Practice shifting and getting used to the amount of time it takes to shift into different gears, especially when shifting the front derailleur. There is a lot of space between those rings, and it takes a lot longer for the gears to engage than on a tightly sprocketed racing bike. Gearing familiarity is important so that you can anticipate gear shifts before you *need* them.

Let's say you are pedaling at a medium speed with the chain in the middle ring up front and your highest gear in back. You see a hill approaching, gentle at the bottom but steep at the top. You start up the hill and begin to shift the rear derailleur into the high gear. The chain clangs and jumps around as you try to apply more power against the shifting gear. Finally the noise ceases as you get the chain into the chosen gear. But it's not enough. The hill has steepened, and you need to be in the smallest front chain ring. So you shift again. You're trying to keep the speed up by applying more power, but it just won't shift. It's rubbing against the front derailleur, making an awful noise. All your friends are passing you, cranking away in their highest gears. Finally the bike slows down, and it shifts. You come to a stop and fall down in utter exhaustion.

Mountain bikes are hard to shift when a lot of force is being applied to the system. They need to jump large gaps, and a lot of tension on the chain bogs them down. By anticipating your gear shifts, you can shift before the force is required. That way the chain is in the proper gear when you need it.

Drive trains are constantly being updated. More and more cogs (gears) are being added every year. Soon mountain bikes may have ten- or eleven-cog freewheels. Chains are narrower to accommodate more gears. If you look closely, you'll see that small scallops have been stamped onto the cogs, which help the chain jump from gear to gear while shifting. The combination of technology helps cyclists shift even while straining up climbs, but even with advanced components, it's still best to anticipate your shifts.

Your friends shifted like this: They saw the hill and shifted into the low gear in the rear sprocket. The chain seated itself in the sprocket as they reached the gentle incline and speed was not lost. Anticipating the steep section, they shifted the front derailleur, losing a little speed, but prepared for the ascent. Now they happily cranked up the hill, actually gaining a little speed as they crested the rise. Once on top they waited for you, as all good friends will do. However, they still poked fun at your lack of shifting skills!

Anticipate gear shifts in changing terrain or obstacles. Know your gearing and shift accordingly. There is nothing worse than hitting a patch of sand in high gear and trying to muscle through it.

Riding Skills   **19**

Get used to turning, braking, slow-speed maneuvering, and shifting before you hit the trail. As your skills develop, go out for short trips on easy trails or roads. Keep your speed down. Once you feel confident, you can get gonzo and hammer!

The Long Ride

Once you are familiar with your mountain bike, it's time to take it in the dirt. Before you go out on your first long ride, there are preparations that must be made. You want to be ready for anything. If your chain breaks 10 miles from the nearest road, if a sudden storm hits, or if you simply get tired, you want to possess certain survival skills that will get you home safely.

What to Take with You and How to Carry It

Obviously you will want to take extra clothes, some food and water, a small repair kit, and perhaps a camera, binoculars, and whatever else you might want to carry with you. There are many options for different types of carriers, the most compact and portable being a small daypack. In choosing a daypack for riding, you'll want one with a narrow profile and a waist strap. The pack should conform to your body and not swing around as you ride. The smaller the better, but make sure it is large enough to hold what you need. A good hydration pack is your best friend, allowing you to carry water, extra clothing, food, and survival gear.

Some feel that a pack gets in the way of their movements on the bike and would rather load up the bike than themselves. There are myriad different bike bags, panniers, water bottle baskets, and carriers. Side panniers, like the ones used in road touring, tend to get in the way on single tracks and may get wet when crossing water. A rear carrier is more practical, and the extra weight back there will add some traction, but it will also degrade the bike's handling if you are riding over anything that requires weight shifts or the ability to get your rear end over the rear wheel. Anything mounted to your bike is going to affect handling in a negative way. A saddlebag is nice for carrying your tool kit, but don't buy a real large one that gets in the way of a bag on the rear carrier.

A handlebar bag is a nice place to carry munchies, a map, and other necessities you may need while riding. Frame bags ride between the down tube and the top tube. But don't load your bike up too much; it'll be a bear on the uphills and will limit technical control over rough terrain. Use good judgment. If you are riding technical terrain and the long ride is made longer by the challenge of difficult terrain, carry as much on your body as is comfortable. If you are riding on smooth fire roads or pavement, you can put more on the bike.

Inside these bags I usually place a rain jacket or windbreaker, tights, some gloves (besides riding gloves), a hat, sunglasses, sun cream, a small first-aid kit, and a cell phone. I bring a lunch or dinner, depending on how long I'm riding, some energy bars, and some munchies. Always bring a lot of water, because you can get dehydrated fast and the majority of natural water supplies are unsafe to drink. A light is a good idea—perhaps a clip-on battery-operated light or a headlamp. Be sure it's bright enough to light your path and can be seen by other vehicles if you plan to be on the road at night.

The Tool Kit

In my tool kit you will find a good multitool designed especially for the mountain biker. These tools are available from a number of manufacturers like Park (the bike tool people), Ritchey, Topeak, and others. The tool should include a usable chain tool, crescent wrench or assortment of box end wrenches, Allen wrenches, screwdrivers, spoke wrenches, and a tire iron. Make sure that you have enough tools to take care of any basic repairs on your specific bicycle. If you find the tool to be lacking a certain Allen wrench, for example, then add that to the kit. Before you depart, test the tool's functionality on all bolts and screws on your bike. Wrap a bit of duct tape around a pen or pencil and include it in your kit. This stuff works for fixing everything from a missing bolt to a laceration. A tire boot is also handy for those sidewall cuts. A dollar bill will work in most situations.

Shoes and Clothes

With the advent of clipless pedals, toe clips are obsolete affairs, but if you are using hiking boots or cross-trainers on your ride to facilitate hiking, then toe clips or flat pedals are an option. Some manufacturers of cycling shoes are now making stout mountain-biking shoes good for hiking that also allow for a cleat in the sole. If you can afford them, go for it. If you are just biking and will not be leaving the bike for a hike, standard mountain-biking shoes with clip-less pedals are best. The best pedal and shoe combination is made by a French company called Time. Ritchey and Shimano also make good pedals. There are many choices, so pick something that is comfortable, sturdy, and reliable. Don't head out onto a long ride with a new set of clipless pedals. Practice first.

Wear clothes designed for mountain biking. Don't wear blue jeans or cotton. Bike clothing is the only way to go for any long ride for safety as well as comfort's sake. These clothes are sometimes padded for the crashes and have chamois cloth where your body comes in contact with the bike. They are breathable and wick away moisture from your skin. Cotton will hold moisture next to your body for that clammy feeling in summer and that hypothermic feeling in winter. High-tech clothing is one of the best things about modern times.

Safety Equipment

A helmet should always be worn while riding. One day I went over the handlebars and landed on my head in soft sand. I got up gig-gling until I saw the basketball size granite boulder half-hidden where my helmetless head hit the dirt. Buy a helmet that is comfortable and fits snugly. Keep it buckled tight but not so tight as to be uncomfortable. An unbuckled helmet will come right off in a fall. If your helmet does come in handy someday, it will probably crack. Throw it away and buy a new one. It has served you well.

On fast descents I'll sometimes wear knee pads or elbow pads. It adds a sense of security when there is a high risk of falling. Even a chest guard isn't a bad idea, although it may sound like a little much. I knew a fella whose handlebars penetrated his belly. The result was a ruptured spleen. A mountain bike can kill you. It is a calculated risk. Minimize injury by keeping your speed down and staying in control.

Lock It Up

If you are riding your bike in the urban jungle, use a lock. U-locks work best when passed through the rear wheel, the frame, and an immovable object. Chains and cable locks can be sliced easily with a pair of bolt cutters. Mountain bikes are the most often stolen bicycle, so *always* lock your bike.

Now, let's go on a ride.

Choose a ride that's not going to kill you. Maps, especially road maps, can be awfully deceiving. Know how to use a topographic map and use it to plan your ride. A topographic map will not only show you elevation, it will show you habitations, four-wheel-drive roads (where you can ride), wilderness areas (where you can't ride), and private land (where you might get shot at). You can see where there are seasonal streams and streams too big to ford. It shows you where there are forests of shade and open views. Topographic maps are essential.

For your first long ride, go up and down the same way. Get an idea of what the terrain will be like on the descent so that there are no surprises. Also, if you grow tired on the uphill, you can simply turn around and go back the way you came. Pick a dirt road as opposed to a trail so that there is less negotiating of obstacles. And pick a classic—perhaps a ride up a canyon or through a forest. Have a destination in mind: a lake, a spectacular view, or maybe just a friend's house. Most of all, have a good time!

After you've accumulated some miles under your belt, challenge yourself. Try a loop trip, riding up to a viewpoint then down to your starting point. Hook up a network of trails, logging roads, or streets to take you a different way to a familiar place. Once you have acquired the skills, there is no end to the fun you can have.

Advanced Skills

You are ready for a long ride. On the way you'll find many challenges, such as hills, descents, and obstacles. In this chapter I will tell you how to master these with grace and finesse. We are now out on some backcountry trails, not tooling around the neighborhood. These skills will allow you to ride safely and efficiently so that you won't hurt yourself, overexert yourself, and swear never to ride a mountain bike again. We want to build your mountain-biking confidence and ability. The idea here is to have fun—and to become accomplished at the skills needed to attain that exalted state.

Uphill

For some, the idea of pedaling a thirty-pound machine up a steep incline does not sound enticing. Many people recall childhood memories of trying to pedal a single-speed bike up a hill and not having much fun doing it.

Yet it is not as bad as it sounds. The mountain bike is designed for ascension; with gearing, weight shifts, and use of certain techniques, hill climbing is easier than you might think.

The gearing arrangement of mountain bikes makes hills easy. On the flats the lowest gears seem ridiculous. You spin and spin and spin but don't seem to go very far. Apply that gearing to a hill, though, and amazing things happen. You seemingly can ascend anything, for hours on end, with very little difficulty. Problems arise as the hill steepens or the terrain changes. But with a little skill and a good attitude, "uphill" translates to fun.

Attitude

First of all, don't look at hill climbing negatively. Approach each hill as your own personal challenge. You're going to get to the top, no matter what. You may have to stop and rest once in a while, even walk the bike, but next time you'll climb this same hill at one clip. Be motivated when you climb hills. The top is your reward.

Keep It Up

You can get motivated by setting up for the hill properly. As you approach the hill, develop a strong spin. As the terrain grows steeper and you must downshift, keep your rpm's up. Anticipate the shift and try not to shift under power. Shift early enough so that you aren't exerting a lot of force to maintain that spin. You should be exerting the same amount of force after the gear change as you did before the gear change. You probably will slow down, but that's OK. The idea is to maintain your rate of spin and exert the same amount of force, no matter which gear you shift into. You want to get up the hill as efficiently as possible.

Keep Going, Even if It's Steep

As the hill gets really steep, you may find yourself in your lowest gear, quickly losing your cadence. You try standing in the saddle but find that the tire skids out in the dirt. Sit down, keep your weight on the rear tire, and lean forward over the bars to keep the front end from coming off the ground. Your weight over the rear wheel adds traction. It also helps to raise your seat for extended climbs and adds more power to the pedals. As you sit on the seat, your knees should be slightly bent (Figure 13).

If the riding surface is firm, you can sometimes stand in the saddle and lean slightly back to add traction. Stay loose and try not to mash too hard on the pedals. An uneven stroke will cause you to lose traction. A good full-suspension bike will keep that rear wheel tracking by making it follow the uneven terrain. This is not something you get on the first ride, so be patient with yourself.

The Line

It is important to pick a good line when climbing. Try to keep the bike as straight as possible. Turning the front wheel from side to side to keep your balance reduces your momentum. Try pulling

Figure 13

Sitting back in the saddle and leaning forward gives more traction

miniwheelies to reduce friction and add even more traction. Look
ahead and try to gauge the terrain before you get there. Avoid loose
dirt, ruts, and roots. If you must climb through them, keep the bike
straight. Full-suspension bikes allow you to get sloppy with your line
and even pick better, more efficient lines over rough terrain. The idea
is to maintain momentum while allotting your energy to places
where spurts of power are needed. Try to relax your upper body;
loosen that death grip on the bars.

Practice

As you try steeper hills with many obstacles, you might get discour-
aged. Keep on trying to ride them as practice, even though you may
have to rest often. A hill that you've ascended many times is always
easier than it was the first time. Apply the techniques you have
learned to steeper and longer climbs.

Starting Up, Again

When you start out on a hill, you must immediately develop a
strong spin to keep the bike going. Get on the bike, place one foot on

the pedal and press down hard. Use the other foot to keep you in balance, then quickly push down on the other pedal. If you stop between strokes, you will instantly lose momentum and lose your balance.

Too Steep

All right, so the hill is just too steep to climb. Go ahead and walk the bike. Sometimes a little walking is what you need to rest up enough so that you can try riding again. But let's face it, some hills are just too steep to ride. Keep walking.

Walking the bike also takes a little skill. Don't walk the bike while straddling the top tube. Get off the bike. Don't push using both handlebars. This is inefficient because all your force is being applied to the front wheel while the rear wheel drags. Hold onto the closest handlebar and the back of the seat. I like to apply most of the force to the rear and just keep the bike straight with the front. This way the front wheel tends to bounce over stones and obstacles while the rear wheel gets lifted over.

If you must carry the bike, hoist it onto your shoulder with one arm and keep the handlebars out of your face with the other arm. Thirty pounds of mountain bike can be a lot to carry over distance, so you may want a shoulder pad. If you are going to carry a heavy bike over an extended section of trail, it may be better to put it on your back. A good pack will soften the effect on your backbone. To do this, stand the bike up, turn away from it, squat down, and pick it up by the top tube with both hands over each shoulder. Stand up and balance the bike on the upper portion of your back. Try to make it feel as though it is inside your backpack. Once the bike is in a comfortable position on your back, start walking.

I know of a ride where 1 mile of walking uphill brings you 9 miles of the best downhill you could imagine. The ascent winds up a steep talus field of boulders and sand. You walk and sometimes carry your bike up. At the top you are greeted by alpine meadows, groves of pines, and firm, level trails. Soon the trail drops back into the canyon, through fields of aspen, granite boulders, and incredible winding roads. It's time to learn some descending skills.

Descending

Descending is the most thrilling and dangerous part of mountain bike riding. Gravity provides the thrill; you provide the skill. The objective: Don't fall down. It is a balancing act. You don't have to go fast. Just stay in control. Speed comes with skill. If you want to go fast, know what you are doing. The expert downhiller is the one who does not get hurt.

If there is one thing to remember about descents, it is to stay in control. You can really push it and hurt yourself badly. Know your ability, your bike, and the descent. Be cautious. You can still go fast, but be reasonable.

First, make sure your bike is in proper working order. Be sure your brakes are tight. Loose brakes might not provide enough braking force and can be forced beneath the rim, rendering the brakes useless. Make sure your shock is adjusted properly. A little spring will help you maneuver over rock and roots, but too much bounce could cause you to lose control. Tighten the quick release on your wheels. Check your derailleurs. The tires should be true. One bump and a wobbly wheel can collapse. This bike is going to be put through some abuse.

Before you start the descent, you might wish to lower your saddle so that you can get farther back on the bike to put more weight on the rear wheel. Your riding stance should be upright and relaxed (Figure 14). Shift slightly to the rear of the seat or slide completely off the seat and balance over the rear wheel to keep traction, and place your pedals horizontally. As you hit bumps and ruts, absorb the shock by rising slightly off the seat. A full-suspension bike will provide more control, but you will still have to use your knees and elbows to absorb a lot of the bumps. Stay loose. Keep a good grip on the handlebars, but don't tense up. The faster you go, the more you want to shift your weight over the rear of the bike.

The majority of the shock will be absorbed by the front suspension shock and at the handlebars, so you want to be sure to keep your hands loose yet firm enough so that the bars don't get jerked out of your hands. Good brakes like discs or V-brakes set at the highest leverage allow you to brake with more control without a death grip on the bars. Setting the brakes at highest leverage also makes them "touchy." A touchy brake will send you over the bars if you are not gentle on the lever. There are many techniques for hand-braking control, but the best is the one that allows you to keep as much of the surface of your hand around the bars as possible (see Figure 9, page 14). A one-finger braking technique is best because you've got

Advanced Skills   **29**

Figure 14

Downhill riding stance

the rest of your fingers wrapped around the bar, but this is also an advanced technique. Most racers use index- or middle-finger techniques. Using the middle finger alone allows you to shift gears while you are braking; this is a braking style used by many pro downhillers.

The best advice is to control your speed. Never let the speed build to a point where you panic and grab the brakes. Stay relaxed and you'll stay in control.

Terrain Changes on Descents

Scan back and forth from what you're riding across to what you're about to ride over. Anticipate your next move. Try to judge the approaching terrain and ride and shift accordingly. Washboards are easy. Keep your weight back and just ride over them. Pinch the front of the seat with your thighs to add stability. Ruts get trickier. Try to stay out of places where water has carved little canyons into the surface. If you find yourself in a rut, don't try to steer out of it immediately. Your front wheel can get stuck and flip you over. Reduce your speed by braking slowly. Look for a place where the sides of the rut are not steep, and exit there. If you can, avoid getting into a rut in the first place.

Gravel and Rocky Roads

Gravelly roads can be scary. You have less traction on gravel yet can travel just as fast as on dirt. Keep your speed down on curves, perhaps going into a controlled skid in the tighter turns. Don't move around a lot while riding gravel. Stand on the pedals and pinch the seat with your thighs. Try to keep the bike riding upright and straight.

Rocky roads hurt. A large rock might impede progress and flip you over. It is often hard to judge how fast you can go through rocky sections. Be cautious. If you enter at a fast rate of speed, sit way back on the seat, almost over the rear tire, gently brake, and ride it out. Braking suddenly can throw you down. Anticipate the terrain, and slow down before you get there.

Steep Descents

Really steep descents call for caution. Roll up to the descent and look over. If it looks too scary, get off and walk down. If you commit, start out as slow as you can and roll into it. Exaggerate the weight shift backward. Stand up on the pedals and put your butt way back behind the saddle. Stay loose. Favor your rear brake; feather your front. Your front brake is where all the power is, but if there are any loose rocks, your front wheel should be moving in order to be able to steer around them. Moving your weight to the extreme rear of the bike will weight the rear wheel to give your rear tire a grip. Control your speed as best you can, favoring the front brake whenever the ground is smooth and the rear when the ground is rocky. Loosen your grip on the brakes to roll through really rough sections.

If it is a short and steep descent, coast through it without braking. Braking suddenly on steep terrain will cause you to fall. Enter the steep section at a safe rate of speed because you will pick up speed as you coast through it.

Sand

Sand can make a bike squirrelly and slow it down instantly. Soft spots will flip you. The best way to approach sand is to maintain a low, rear-weighted stance, as in riding rocky sections. The important thing is to keep the bike straight while riding through the sand.

Figure 15
....
Riding through sand

Search for someone else's rut and put your wheels in it. Try not to steer with the bars, but rather with your hips and shoulders. Move your weight very far back over the rear wheel. Extend your arms like Superman. Do *not* use your front brake! Pull back on the bars as though you are hanging onto a railing. Float (Figure 15).

Obstacles on Descents

Be aware of obstacles in the roadway and to the sides. A branch can get stuck in your spokes. Hidden holes will toss you to the ground. It may be difficult to see obstacles as you go in and out of the shade. Adjust your speed so that you can be totally aware of changes in terrain. Also, watch what is to the sides of the road. If you must make a quick evasive maneuver, you don't want to hit a tree or a boulder.

Be committed as you ride through obstacles. You either have to blast over them or slow down and safely negotiate them. Keep looking ahead of you—keeping your weight back and your stance low and being prepared for anything. To get through a particularly rough section of trail, do not use your brakes. If this will cause you to accelerate to a speed where you will be beyond your skills or control, get off *before* the rough stretch.

Cornering on Descents

Corners can be tricky on descents. The two most frequently made mistakes are overshooting the corner and skidding out or flipping from improper weight distribution. As you enter the corner, look ahead and try to judge how fast you can take it and where your line will be in order to maintain speed. Scrub off speed before you enter the corner and lean (not steer) toward the apex of the turn. Be sure your pedals are aligned vertically, with the downward pedal toward the outside of the turn. Put your weight on the outside pedal—put *no* weight on the inside pedal. The feeling you will get as you round the turn is as though you are squashing a bug with your outside foot. Do not weight the outside handlebar grip. Put a little weight onto the inside grip, pointing toward the turn. You should have slowed to a reasonable speed prior to the apex of the turn. Let go of the brake as you reach the apex, make the turn, stand the bike up, and then accelerate out, if you can. Keep your chain in the biggest chain ring. This will keep the chain from bouncing and chipping paint off your frame. It will also keep the ring's teeth from biting into your leg if you crash.

At the apex of the turn there are many different techniques you can use. You can take a tighter line and brake hard, skidding out the rear wheel at the apex. This is an environmentally incorrect move, however, especially on a tight single track that can be damaged by this kind of use. On a dirt road, though, this is a lot of fun. Another way to do it is to take an outside line, describing a larger arc, then drop into the apex with a straight line through the turn. Likewise, you can come into the apex on a straight track, then skid or turn out on the outside of the turn. Your choice depends on the terrain in the turn and your speed as you enter the turn.

If it is soft on the outside of a turn, drop into the apex to avoid it. If it's soft at the apex, a tight turn may be warranted to blast through it. If you are entering a pair of S-curves, a straight line as you exit the turn will set you up for the next curve (Figure 16).

Advanced Skills   **33**

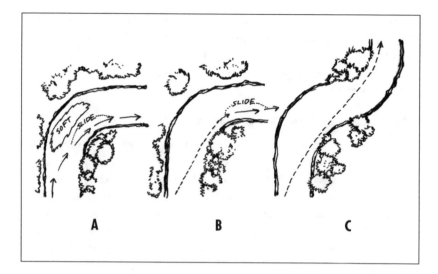

Figure 16

A) Outside turn
B) Inside turn
C) S-curve—choose a straight line

Out of Control

So you're bombing down a hill and suddenly find yourself out of control. The best thing to do is to try to slow down without skidding. Brake slowly and try to keep the bike riding on a straight line, even if it means riding off the road. A sudden turn may tumble you. If wrecking is imminent, let go of your bike, tuck, and roll. Avoid putting one arm down to stop your fall.

To avoid a wreck, slow down to a complete stop and start over. You might think you have reduced your speed enough without stopping, only to find yourself out of control again. Stop and catch your breath. Always be cautious on descents.

Just because it's a descent doesn't mean you have to go fast. But if you are going to fly down hills, know some technique. Practice descending while wearing knee pads, elbow pads, and a helmet. As you get better, push it a little. But always stay in control. Use these techniques to keep upright and have fun!

Obstacles

Mountain bikes are unbelievable tools that can ride over logs, across boulders, and into streams. It takes a little skill but is a wonderful talent that can be mastered with little difficulty. To become skilled at obstacles, know the limitations of your bike and what it needs to clear certain obstacles.

First, be sure to have the proper safety equipment when riding over obstacles. Riding obstacles is a delicate balancing act that can result in injury. Always wear a helmet and maybe even knee pads and elbow pads. Put some knee pads around your shins. Sometimes your feet slip off the pedals and the pedals can strike your shins. Minor corrections can be made with an outstretched leg or arm pushing off on a tree or a rock. In a complete rollover, try to get away from the obstacle and the bike. Falling from atop an obstacle can be devastating.

Before you try riding obstacles, gain an understanding of how a bike clears an obstacle. Get off your bike and walk it over the obstacle. Watch where the bicycle clears an obstacle and where it does not. Understand the forces involved in getting it up and over.

The Log

The most basic obstacle is the log. A small log is easy to negotiate. Pull a small wheelie over the log and throw your weight forward to get the rear wheel over the log. As you come off the log, shift your center of gravity to the rear of the bike (Figure 17). Obstacles can be broken into three parts: enough speed to get up, enough momentum to get over the apex, and proper weight distribution to descend. These principles can be applied to any obstacle.

35

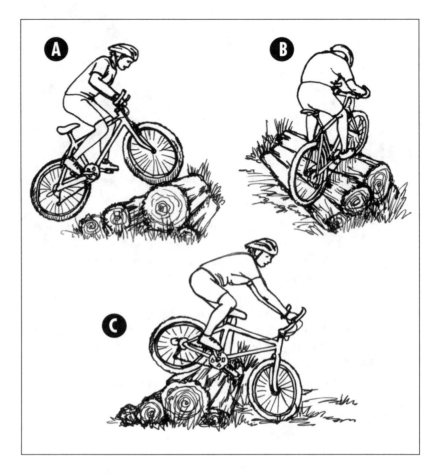

Figure 17

Log-crossing sequence

> A) Pop a wheelie to place the front wheel on the log.
> B) Throw your weight forward to bring the back wheel on the log.
> C) Put your weight back and ride off.

Try walking the bike over a larger log (about 12 to 24 inches in height). Lift gently on the handlebars and bring the front wheel over the log. It will look like the chain ring is about to hit the top of the log. But as the front wheel descends one side of the log, the rear wheel has already begun to rise above the log, clearing the chain ring. On a smaller log, the front wheel will be on the ground before the rear wheel can get up the log and the chain ring will not clear. Obviously, the larger the log, the easier it will be to clear the chain ring. The problem lies in getting up on the log in the first place.

It takes a lot of force to get up on the log. Ride toward it at a good clip and pull a wheelie, landing your front wheel atop the log. At this point, your bike will come to a complete stop—unless you throw your weight forward with the momentum of the bike. This pushes the bike over the log and brings your rear wheel atop the log. It's important to breathe out and relax at this point. Stalling and tensing up almost guarantee crashing from the top of the obstacle.

You want to be sure that your pedals are set upright as you mount the log. Keep them vertical as you pull the wheelie and push them to horizontal at the exact moment you throw your weight forward. Do not pedal to vertical, as your pedal is sure to hit the log. Once your front wheel is over the log, begin pedaling again.

As you descend, you want to shift your weight back so that you don't flip over the front. Sit back as far as possible behind the seat, so that your rear end is almost touching the rear tire. Your center of gravity should be over the obstacle as you ride over it. Once on the ground, center yourself back over the bike.

Momentum and balance must work together in clearing obstacles. You need enough momentum to get over the obstacle while at the same time keeping your balance. Too little momentum will stop you; too much and it's dirt for lunch. As you practice you'll get an idea of what it takes to get you up and over.

Another technique is to grind the teeth of your chain ring into the log and pedal over it. Although this technique is effective on flatter logs, it's sure to damage your chain ring. Any way you look at it, you are bound to hit your chain ring practicing obstacles. Look at your chain ring as a disposable item; buy cheap ones if you will be attempting obstacles. I replace my chain ring every few months.

Hopping over a Log

As the log gets bigger, it is more difficult to get enough momentum to get atop it. The hopping technique may be used to get you up and over a log that is bigger than the bike itself, although the technique is very difficult to master (especially with a full-suspension bike). Hopping differs from the techniques just described because

Figure 18

Clearing a big log

the cyclist does not ride up and over the obstacle in one continuous motion. In hopping, momentum is broken down into moves, each move concentrating on getting a certain part of the bike up and over the log one move at a time.

Crucial to this technique is the ability to balance the bike between moves. To do this, the bike must be completely stationary. This technique is as difficult to master as hopping, but it is essential in getting over large obstacles. It is a technique that must be practiced and built upon, first by riding to a complete stop and attempting to balance. It is easier to balance if the bike is moving slightly. Pedal a little, then stop, shifting your weight backward. Once mastered, you will be able to integrate balancing with hopping to clear large obstacles.

To clear a large log, you must pull a wheelie and land the front wheel atop the log, pulling on the brakes to stop the bike from falling backward off the log (Figure 18). Now push your momentum forward, and hop the rear wheel on top of the log, again braking and remaining stationary atop the log. Now, ride off the log with your weight as far back as possible. It's much easier said than done.

The Log Bridge

A log bridge is scary yet not as difficult as it looks. Approach the log at a good clip, and get both wheels onto it steering straight. Continue to pedal the length of the log, keeping the front wheel straight. Balance comes from forward inertia, not your steering ability. So be sure to be in a gear that is applying power to the bike and not just coasting across. If you feel as though you are going to fall, try to get away from the bike.

These techniques have advanced into a subsport of mountain biking called "trials." Trials riding involves mastering such obstacles as boulders, cars, and picnic tables—all while keeping your feet clipped in or balanced on the pedals. Blending the techniques of freestyle trick riding and mountain biking, trials is far removed from what we might encounter in our daily mountain bike excursion. Trials riders are able to hop up an obstacle and jump off from 10 feet up, completing a full 360-degree rotation before landing. Since trials is really a completely different sport from mountain biking, this book will not attempt to describe the more advanced techniques of trials riding, even though they can be performed on a mountain bike.

Hopping and standing, however, are techniques you can use in your everyday rides. Perfecting these techniques will make obstacles easier, especially when you're attempting boulders and other rock obstacles.

Boulders, Rocks, and Hard Knocks

Boulders are approached just like logs, except for one difference: Boulders are not as uniform, hence they can be more difficult. In going over large boulders, I scout out all sides of the rock, looking for the lowest angled side. I ascend on this side and descend a steeper side (Figure 19). Avoid riding over the summit of the boulder and descending. You are bound to hit the chain ring on the summit.

Instead, look for a place where the boulder flattens out before steepening for the descent.

Often the ascent and descent of the boulder will not be in a straight line, so a small turn may have to be made. Make this turn by steering, not leaning. Try to keep your balance as upright as possible to avoid falling off the boulder.

On large boulders that you must go up and over, it is best to be in a low gearing, but not so low that your pedal strokes won't provide enough power to get you up and over the boulder. And remember to align your pedals where clearance might be a problem. Keeping them horizontal as you go over the top is best.

On smaller boulders, backpedaling helps to give you clearance. A full rotation may cause a pedal to strike the rock. Place your pedals horizontally where you need clearance, then pedal a half stroke to

Figure 19

Riding over boulders

give you power. Backpedal one-half revolution to avoid striking the pedal, then pedal forward over the rock. This way, you avoid striking the pedal on the rock while at the same time giving power to the bike.

Pedals are another disposable item. Like it or not, they get pretty bashed up. Some pedals are quite sturdy and take a lot of abuse. However, in a severe impact, some pedals may bend within the crank and pull out, stripping the crank or breaking off in the crank themselves. Some cyclists use less cumbersome clipless pedals. Since these pedals are smaller, the shoe will frequently glance off the rock instead of the pedal. I use plastic pedals that simply break upon impact. When there is not enough pedal to stand on, I throw them away. You may not be so harsh on your pedals and prefer a sturdy metal pedal. Equipment choice is a matter of personal preference.

You might have to ride through a series of large rocks. It is a matter of picking the best line to get through the obstacle. Try to weave the front tire through rocks and let the rear tire ride up and over them. This requires standing up on the pedals and throwing your weight forward as the rear tire hits the rock. Sometimes you can aim it just right so that the front wheel passes to one side of the rock, the chain ring passes over the rock, and the rear wheel passes to the opposite side.

Water

Water crossings are fun. They'll cool you off on that long, hot ride—without getting your feet wet. The bike actually carves a path through the water, spraying your torso and keeping your feet dry. However, one mistake in a water crossing and you might get more than just your feet wet.

Examine the water crossing carefully before attempting it. Hidden boulders or sudden deep spots can sink you. Some water crossings appear at pools in the streams and have similar characteristics. The water is dammed by boulders and rocks on the downstream side of the pool. Sand collects against these rocks, with other rocks lying against the upstream side of the pool. You want to avoid hitting any large rocks as you go through the pool; likewise, you do not want to get bogged down in the sand. The best place to cross is that point between sand and rocks, where the bottom of the stream is consistent and smooth.

Approach the stream at a good rate of speed, coasting into it. The water will slow you down considerably. As your speed drops, start pedaling. Be sure that you are in a low gear, but not so low that you can't get any power. Keep your weight over the rear tire for maximum traction. As you begin to rise out of the stream, drop to a lower gear and stand up as you gain traction on dry ground.

A very fast rate of speed will cause the bike to hydroplane on the water, actually skim across the surface. This is very dangerous, for you really do not have any control over the bike until you've reached dry ground on the other side. Try riding through streams before attempting to hydroplane the bike.

Most mountain bikes are equipped with sealed-bearing hubs and bottom brackets that keep moisture out of these areas. If your bike does not have a sealed system, riding through water can hurt the bike. The grease inside will run out of the hubs and your bearings will be grinding against the unlubricated axle. In nonsealed bearing systems, never immerse the bottom bracket or hubs totally in the water.

Snow and Ice

Where I live, 20-foot snowstorms are not uncommon. With that much snow, the plows have a tough time keeping the roads clear. Autos are marooned, yet mountain bikes flourish. The snow provides unbelievable traction. When things get icy, though, it gets dangerous. If you hit a patch of ice and you feel the bike starting to go, place both feet firmly on the ice and let the bike fall from beneath you. Balance on your feet and skate out of it. This is strictly a survival technique and is difficult to perform successfully. Try to avoid riding on ice to begin with.

Although rocks, logs, and water are the most common obstacles when trail riding, there are others. Curbs, drains, cars, dogs, and potholes are more urban types of obstacles. These will be dealt with in another chapter. But the approach is similar. You can use the same technique for descending stairs as you do for descending a boulder. Just be safe when attempting obstacles. Scout the obstacle, wear safety gear, and don't get in over your head or you might land on it. Be safe—and have fun.

All-Terrain

The term "mountain bike" is incorrect. These bikes are not exclusive to the mountains. They are perfect for city riding, across the farm, or along the beach. They are really all-terrain bikes, also known as ATBs. Mountain bikes can be ridden over many types of terrain, and the handling characteristics change for each type of terrain encountered. In this chapter we will discuss the differences between riding a trail and a road, over slick rock or the beach, and the places you should not ride—like over the neighbor's lawn, for instance.

Mountain-Bike Etiquette

Many people perceive mountain bikes as destructive machines bombing across country, scaring wildlife and livestock, and wreaking havoc upon all who come in their path. Unfortunately, there are all kinds of people on mountain bikes these days, and sometimes this reputation is warranted. But mostly the fear of mountain bikes by those who do not ride them is exaggerated. Undoubtedly, you will encounter people in the backcountry who may harbor ill will against you. Or perhaps they have never seen a mountain bike, and this is your chance to educate them.

A code of proper behavior on a mountain bike has been created for you to follow. Abide by these guidelines, because you are an ambassador of mountain biking. Demonstrate that mountain bikes and mountain bikers are not the vermin of the backcountry.

The mountain biker's code, as defined by the National Off-Road Bicyclist Association (NORBA), is as follows:

1) I will yield the right of way to other nonmotorized recreationalists.

2) I will use caution when overtaking another and will make my presence known well in advance.

3) I will maintain control of my speed at all times.

4) I will stay on designated trails.

5) I will not disturb wildlife and livestock.

6) I will not litter.

7) I will respect public and private property.

8) I will always be self-sufficient.

9) I will not travel solo when bikepacking in remote areas.

10) I will observe the practice of minimum-impact bicycling.

11) I will always wear a helmet when I ride.

Single Track

Treat the land and those who use it with respect. This means minimum impact. Pick up your garbage, don't pollute streams and lakes with soap and wastes, and never ride across meadows or fields. Where animals are grazing, always close gates behind you and stay away from the livestock. Mountain bikes already have restricted access to many places. Let's show the public that we care.

Trails have become known as single tracks in mountain-bike jargon. Dirt roads, with their dual grooves, are double tracks, although they are not regularly called this. The single track provides some of the most exciting riding for a couple of reasons. First, you are not going to encounter any automobiles on the single track and, depending on where you ride, maybe no motorcycles either. The single track tends to be more technical because of its narrowness and limited line of sight. You need to keep your speed down on single tracks because a surprise obstacle or hiker might mean a nasty collision.

Single tracks may be a trail in your local park or a hiking trail in the mountains. Before you begin, find out if it is legal to ride a mountain bike on the trail. Many parks, national forests, and recreation areas have banned mountain bikes on their trails. There are many reasons; the most often cited are conflicts with other trail users, like hikers or horses, and trail erosion. Conflicts can be mitigated by careful riding, keeping your speed down, and being aware of other trail users. In fact, on trails where there are other users, I find it best to dismount and let them pass as a courtesy. Put your best foot forward so that other trail users don't get a bad impression of mountain bikers.

Do mountain bikes cause erosion? Yes, but if ridden correctly a mountain bike can be far more environmentally friendly than horses and off-road vehicles, which can cause sand and ruts, even downright destruction of the trail and the ensuing creation of another alongside. Skidding a mountain bike around a turn, riding a wet trail, and traveling off-trail are the worst things we can do to single tracks as mountain bikers.

Currently, many trails are closed to mountain bikes that should not be. Write your congressional representative or park manager. To ban mountain bikes from all trails is discrimination. Arguably there are trails on which mountain bikes should not be allowed, but due to the equestrian lobby and a view by organizations such as the Sierra Club that the mountain bike should be grouped with motorized travel, the case can be made that mountain bikes are mostly misunderstood. As our numbers grow, we will have more power, but we will also be much more of a destructive force in wilderness. By being responsible, we might be able to stem the political tide in coming years and find our niche along with the horses and the jeeps. The most important rule to follow at this point is only to ride on trails that are open to us.

Once you've determined that it's legal to ride on the trail, determine who else might be using it. Horses and bikes are usually a bad mix. Horses spook easily and are unpredictable at best. If you ride a trail that's also open to horses, keep your speed down at all times and give them every kind of right of way you can. If you come up on a horse from the rear, make sure you talk as you approach so that the horse is not startled. Ask the rider to allow you to pass if there is room to go around. Be courteous and try to make a good impression. Equestrians will appreciate your efforts. If a horse is coming at you, dismount and get as far off the trail as you can to allow the horse to pass. Don't resume your ride until the horse is out of range. Increase your speed only when you have good view. As you approach corners, slow down. Often corners will be tight, so you will want to keep it slow anyway.

You'll often find the center of the trail very sandy. Ride up on the edge of the trail where it is more compact, taking care not to ride *off* the trail. Where there is a water bar in the trail (a stone or log placed across the trail to divert runoff), ride over the water bar, not off the trail around it. Never ride off the trail. This *does* create erosion.

There may be branches or plants leaning into the trail. Be careful. A branch can easily put your eye out. Duck down as you approach these obstacles. A branch at handlebar height really hurts when it swipes the hand. Although gloves help, practice riding with one hand and lifting the other hand out of the way. But watch it. You can easily fall riding one-handed.

Switchbacks

Single tracks will often have switchbacks, places where the trail switches directions as it traverses a slope (Figure 20). The switch-back is difficult to ride around. Going upward, you might give the bike a lot of power and abruptly stop pedaling as you start to make your turn. Turn the front wheel 45 degrees to the bike and start ped-aling again. The key here is to slow down enough to make that tight turn. If you're going too fast, the front wheel will dig in and you'll stop. If you are going too slow, you'll fall over.

Going down the switchback is trickier. The same principle applies; however, if you lean too far forward, you will flip over the handlebars. You need to keep your weight back as you slow down for the turn, then lean into the turn once you've turned the handlebars. Keep the brakes on, letting them out in spurts as you go around the switchback.

The single track is a wonderful part of mountain biking. Just be sure you are allowed on the trail and that you don't ruin any other trail user's day. Keep your speed down, especially when visibility is limited.

Dirt Roads

Dirt roads can be just as enjoyable as single tracks. Many forests have logging roads that wind around forever. But don't become a mem-ber of the dead-end gang. Many logging roads will lead to dead-ends that may be agonizing to retrace. Have a map with you, especially on logging roads.

The age-old question concerning dirt roads is "Which track do I ride in?" You want to avoid riding in loose sandy soil and stick to the

Figure 20

Switchback turn

track that has firm and compacted dirt. Sand and debris collect
where the flow of water is impeded. Hence the lower of the two
tracks will usually have silt and debris in it. The higher track will be
more compact and easier to ride in. Also, the steeper the track, the
more compact it is likely to be, with sand piling up at the bottom of
hills. Beware of this sudden sandbox.

To pick the perfect line on a double track, you must be looking
ahead, scanning the terrain. If a soft spot or a pile of rocks lies within
your track, be ready to switch tracks. The center of the road between
tracks is often soft and covered in brush. At high speeds, the center
will catch your front wheel and throw you to the ground. Try to pick
a place to cross the center that seems less brushy and more compact. Turn diagonally and ride a straight line through it. Do not turn
across the center, and try to hit any ruts or rises perpendicular or as

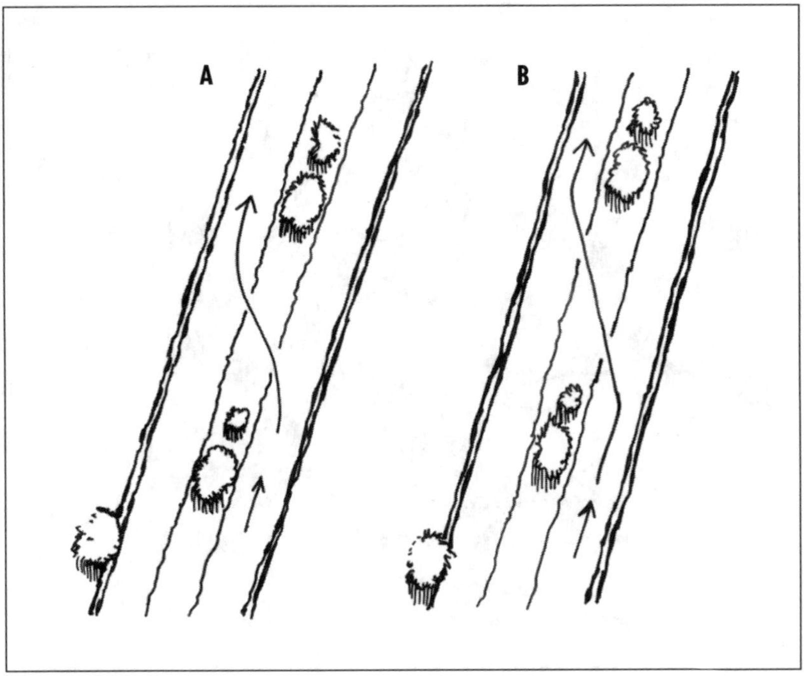

Figure 21

Dirt-road track switch
   A) No
   B) Yes

close to head-on as you can. Start your turn in one track, ride diagonally across the center, and make your next turn after you enter the new track (Figure 21).

Slickrock

Slickrock is a unique geological phenomenon that occurs in sandstone. Erosion has created smooth hills and bowls interspersed with an occasional patch of sand. The landscape is eerie and strange, yet great to ride on.

The Slickrock Trail in Moab, Utah, is a mountain biker's classic. Originally created for motorcycles, the trail has become a mountain-biking mecca. A dashed white line is painted on the surface of the rock for the length of the trail. The trail winds up, down, and around a sandstone plateau above the translucent Colorado River. Along the way, you pass by Indian petroglyphs, delicate wind-sculpted arches, and outstanding views of canyon country.

Riding on slickrock can be compared to riding on pavement, but this natural pavement is much more convoluted. The traction is incredible, but beware of rain or ice. Wet sand on your tires also can make the traction vanish very quickly. Using correct braking technique will allow you to go down slopes that are seemingly impossible, and correct weight distribution will allow you to climb hills that will bust your lungs before your tires break loose.

When going down, use the front brake as you would on a road bike, favoring it over the rear. The front brake is your best friend on slickrock, but keep your weight behind the saddle. The steeper the hill, the farther back you want to be.

When going up, lean out over the front of the bike. Don't worry about traction in the rear; just try to keep the front end of the bike on the ground. Use a slightly higher gear than you think you should, and power up with smooth, strong pedal strokes.

Moab is not the only place you'll find slickrock. Similar formations can be found all over the country on granite and limestone. These techniques will help you wherever the surface is extremely hard and smooth.

Sand, Pumice, and Other Nasties

There is only one good thing that can be said about riding in sand: When you fall, it's a soft landing. Otherwise, sand can be very difficult to ride in. Everyone rides through patches of sand once in a while, but what do you do when the entire trail is one big sand trough? Pick another trail.

Seriously, some of us are not blessed with trails that are always firm. You may live near a beach, in a desert, or close to a volcanic area that has a lot of pumice sand. Riding on these surfaces takes patience and determination. Sand creates a lot of resistance against the bike. The idea is to minimize that resistance.

Always try to keep a straight line when riding through the sand. The more you move around, the more resistance you create against the sand, decreasing efficiency. Sit as far back on the bike as you can, keeping your weight over the rear wheel. This is one time when riding in a rut is a good thing. If you follow an existing rut, your tire will sink down to harder soil. Let the bike follow the rut, and try not to steer.

When it really gets deep, you may try pulling little wheelies. This decreases resistance by pulling the front wheel momentarily out of the sand. Keep pumping. No one said that riding the soft stuff was easy.

Descents in sand can be tricky. Again, maintain a straight line. Don't make sudden movements, especially in curves. Make your turns fluid and wide. Be prepared for variations in the sand. Deep sand will slow you down instantly, possibly throwing you off the bike. By keeping your weight to the rear of the bike and riding a straight line, you can plow through deep sand without incident.

On climbs, the same rules apply. Ride a straight line and keep your weight to the rear by sitting down. Standing out of the saddle is ineffective. Keep it up. Determination and patience are the best techniques you can use in sand.

The Urban Jungle

The majority of mountain bikes will be used in the canyons of the city, on rivers of pavement, and through forests of automobiles and pedestrians. The mountain bike is well suited for the city; potholes, curbs, and sewer grates can be handled with ease. With all the controls at your fingertips, increased stability, and a high point of view, the mountain bike is perfect for city riding.

The first rule of city riding is to be seen. Wear bright clothing or have an antenna flag so that cars can see you. At night have reflective clothing as well as rear and front lights. Remember that traffic is usually traveling at two or three times the speed you are. Signal your intentions well with hand signals *before* you make the move. Avoid riding in a car's blind spot: the right rear corner of an automobile. Always be ready to make an evasive maneuver. Often cars don't know you are there until it is too late.

Awareness is important in city riding. Look to all sides, or have a rearview mirror. At intersections, be aware of the right-turner. He or she will cut you off, crushing your front wheel—or worse. In slow traffic it is best to stay ahead of a car, where you can be seen, or well behind a car, where you have time to get out of the way.

In most states the bike has the same rights and responsibilities as automobiles do. That means obeying all traffic rules. Remember that pedestrians always have the right of way in crosswalks. However, if you are riding in a crosswalk, you do not have the same rights as pedestrians unless you are walking the bike. This is the only time a cyclist can be considered a pedestrian.

Always stay to the far right of the roadway. If you are holding up a line of cars, pull off the road. After all, you are on a mountain bike. Treat the shoulder as another type of terrain!

Obstacles like curbs, stairs, and puddles can be treated the same as logs, boulders, and water crossings. But one of the greatest obstacles in city riding is the unleashed dog. The best way to handle a violent canine is ignorance and speed. Do not heed his barks—and keep pedaling. Once you've passed his territory, he'll give up. Just keep your eyes ahead of you and not on the jaws nipping at your heels.

Occasionally these animals must be taught a lesson. Stopping the bike a safe distance and holding your ground often scares a dog into complacency. A swipe with your pump should be used only in the most extreme instances of self-defense. A good and very effective remedy is a squirt gun filled with ammonia. Carrying a couple of dog biscuits with you is a friendlier tactic. If you are bitten, report the incident to local animal control authorities and have the bite looked at by a doctor.

Always lock your bike in the city. Leave it alone for a second and it's gone. Be careful in rough neighborhoods. I once had a gang of cyclists come up to me and claim that I was riding "their" bike. I held my ground and like the excited canine, they left me alone.

Riding a bike around a city is the best way to get to know it. Stick to bike paths, if possible. Many chambers of commerce have bike maps for cities that show the best routes. Go to the museum, to the park, or to work on your bike and have fun!

Competition

Mountain-bike racing consists of a variety of events: downhills, hill-climbs, observed trials, circuit races, dual challenge (like a slalom ski race), and cross-country races. In most races anyone can participate. You are categorized by your racing experience, age, and type of bike. The different classes are Beginner (never have raced), Intermediate (have raced five races), Expert (have placed in three races or have six top finishes in six races), Super (top-level amateurs), Single Speed Bike, Stock Bike (Trials), Modified Bike (Trials), Junior (under age eighteen), Veteran (ages thirty-five to forty-five), and Masters (age forty-five and up). You can be classified in three categories in each event; e.g., Single Speed, Expert, Masters.

Mountain-bike racers have become specialists in certain events. Some are better hill climbers; others love the downhill. Observed trials riding has really become a separate sport from mountain-bike racing, and many racers prefer not to enter this event. This has led to two methods of scoring events. The first method scores each event individually. In other words, your place on the downhill will have no effect on your place in the cross-country.

The second method of scoring is the stage race. The stage race is where you combine your score in each race to come up with an overall winner for the event. Regardless of how the winner is determined, most mountain-bike racers will agree that winning isn't everything. Mountain-bike competition is a friendly gathering where everyone helps one another. The World Mountain Bike championships held in Mammoth Lakes, California, is one example.

The Hill Climb

I once rode this climb for a pleasure ride. It was *not* pleasurable. The road surface is thick pumice and volcanic rock, making traction difficult. I frequently got off my bike and walked. I would get back on the bike, pedal for a few hundred yards, and feel the thin air of altitude burn in my lungs. I made it, though, riding my bike up and over the rock cairn that marked the 11,053-foot summit. So I didn't *ride* it the entire way, but I *did* finish it. The view from the top was well worth the effort.

But for the race, things are different. The road has been graded and everyone is conditioned to the altitude after a season of racing. The start gun goes off and the racers charge out at 25 miles per hour. They stay in a close pack, take advantage of one another's draft, and exchange the lead to give everyone an equal advantage.

The strategy for a hill climb is to pace yourself so that you don't get too tired before the top. This is one bike race where drafting comes into play. Tucking yourself in behind other riders decreases wind resistance, providing more power. If you are like I am, you won't be able to keep up with the pack and will find yourself strung out along the course. Don't push yourself. Get into a rhythm, enjoy the views, and just finish the race.

The Cross-Country Race

The cross-country race at Mammoth is really a circuit race, although it travels across the countryside. You rise 500 feet in 2 miles to Reds Lake, spin around the lake, and gain the single track for 2 miles along the rim of the San Joaquin River Valley. Then the single track makes a sharp descent, winding around thick Jeffrey pines to the finish. At the finish you are greeted by a large bump that will send you flying. The pros and experts run five circuits, while the amateur riders go around three times.

At the start, everyone is together in a pack. But by Reds Lake the pros and experts have left the amateur riders far behind. No one expects the sharp turn at Reds Lake. Many of the amateur riders are sent over their handlebars into the water. On the single track, the action is fast and furious. Riders bomb through the woods at 40 miles per hour, then stop and push their bikes up the next hill. The descent on the backside is equally as hair-raising. The twisting course demands a tight line and a keen eye, lest you become emblazoned on the bark of a pine tree.

Ned Overend pulled away from the pack at Reds Lake, followed by John Tomac. At the end of the first lap, the two were far from the pack and soon lapped amateur riders. They politely asked the cyclists to move out of the way so that they could move through, and the cyclists complied.

Suddenly, Ned heard the hissing of air and pulled out with a flat, to be passed by Tomac and the pack. Unlike road racing, there was no free lap for technical difficulty. Ned had to fix the tire as quickly as possible and get back in the race, fighting his way back up to the front. This rule illustrates a verity of mountain-bike riding: self-sufficiency. If you are out there and something goes wrong, you'd better be prepared.

Unfortunately, some beginner riders did not understand the camaraderie of mountain-bike racing as Tomac tried to make his way to the front. On the single track, where passing is almost impossible, these riders would not let Tomac pass! Although Tomac finished the race, he did not place because of the insensitivity of some riders. Although a leading rider "owns the track," you always let a stronger rider pass; it is an unwritten rule.

On the last lap, Overend regained the lead and finished in first. He won because he played his cards right. He was prepared with tool kit and tire repair. He passed riders where the road was wide, and held his ground in the single track. His excellent handling skills and boundless energy enabled him to fight his way back to the front. In cross-country races, it is best to hang back and save it up for the end—hoping you don't run into technical trouble. If you do, you must be prepared.

The Dual Challenge

A ski area has a lot of earth-moving equipment to build ski runs, so why not build a race course for mountain bikes? This course has been designed specifically for this event and will be removed once the race is over. The dual challenge starts with two starting gates on a blue and a red course. The riders race against one another through a series of elimination rounds, switching courses each time. The winner is the rider who has won the most races.

The dual challenge brings every mountain-bike skill into one fast race. Shifting, descents, climbing, obstacles, and curves present themselves at the same time. The major difficulty is shifting. Racers must jump between high and low gears in a matter of seconds, while handling their bikes around turns and over bumps. Often racers find themselves trying to crank up the hill in a high gear because they didn't shift in time. Bike handling is a given. You are supposed to be able to negotiate the obstacles. It doesn't always work out that way. Crashes are bound to happen, making this an exciting race to watch.

The Observed Trials

Negotiating obstacles is an obvious component of mountain biking. Observed trials arose out of this necessity. Cyclists test their handling skills through a series of obstacles that mimic the obstacles they might encounter in the woods.

However, as skill levels increased, the obstacles became more outrageous. A skilled trials rider of today would make quick work of a Volkswagen Beetle—riding up its bumper to the hood, hopping onto the roof, then descending the engine cover.

Each movement of the trials rider is observed by a judge, hence the name "observed trials." The rider negotiates a series of obstacles called a section. The goal is to "clean" the section—complete it without putting a foot down, called a "dab." Each dab represents a point. Five points are given for putting your foot down and impeding forward motion. The rider with the lowest number of points is the winner.

Obviously, a bicycle that is designed for trials riding will fare a lot better than the average mountain bike. Trials bikes resemble BMX or freestyle bikes. They are lightweight, with a small chain ring for clearance. Some don't even have a seat, for the trials rider rarely sits down. They have short stubby handle bars and fat tires that are almost fully deflated. These features allow the trials rider to hop the bike easier, clear obstacles, and remain stationary longer.

In most races they have two categories of trials entrants: stock bikes and modified trials bikes. Different courses are designed for each. The stock bike course tends to go through streams and over logs and boulders. The modified bike course is the eye-catcher. It may contain huge boulders as tall as a man, bridges composed of loose bouncing boards, and leaps to the ground from 15 feet up. These are accomplished smoothly with perhaps an extra twist thrown in for show.

In some ways the stock course gets back to the original concept of mountain biking. It's you and the bike out there, and you've got to get through that obstacle alive. When you encounter a log in the woods, you don't switch bikes and start hopping over it; you make do with what you have. In Crested Butte, Colorado, the trials course is completely natural. It is held in an aspen grove outside of town. The sections thread between tight trees, balance across a log bridge, or slosh up a boulder-filled creek. A modified trials bike here would be a disadvantage.

The Kamikaze! Downhill

When the Kamikaze! was first held, no one was sure what the outcome would be. Would the course be littered with bruised bodies and bloody bikes? Would the winners be deranged thrill-seekers with a death wish? As it turned out, relatively few accidents occurred in comparison with other bicycle races. Those who wanted just to complete the course held their speed down; those who wanted to win let it all hang out.

Jim Deaton, a pro rider, was the winner of the first Kamikaze! DH. Considered the best downhiller of his day, his skill and attitude got him down the course safely. Behind him were two local boys who worked at the ski lift and practiced the downhill daily after work.

You get to the top of the course on an aerial tram, the gondola. A start ramp sits a few yards from the actual summit. You mount the ramp with your bike and get ready for the ride of your life.

"Racer ready! Get set! GO!" Down the ramp onto a wide run, you pass ski runs with names like "Hangman's Hollow" and "Wipeout." The dirt is loose, the terrain is steep, and it's tough to keep your bike upright. Sit back, keep a straight line, pinch your seat with your thighs, and hold on tight.

The Kamikaze! downhill is the place to go fast on your bike, not on the trails in your neighborhood. It is reckless and unforgiving. You can get killed doing this. Be sure that you have as much protective clothing on as possible, including a helmet. You can practice for this kind of event on an isolated road that you know is free of traffic. If you are going to commit hara-kiri, just be sure that you don't take anyone else along with you. With the growth of mountain-biking technology, the DH has become an extreme sport where racers are tested by much more than speed. The courses have become obstacle runs through boulders, wet roots, and deep ruts on narrow single tracks as steep and twisting as you can imagine. Full-suspension bikes that are used strictly for DH now have upwards of 8 inches of travel and more closely resemble motorcycles than mountain bikes. The very best thing about all of this excitement and danger is the trickle-down of the technology into the basic lines of the mountain bikes available in your local bike shop.

Times have changed since the first races in Marin County and days that saw the Kamikaze! DH as the pinnacle of the sport. Long ago the race was the thing, the competition was friendly, and the event was a kick. Now racing is serious, and the friendly attitude that used to prevail is fading as fast as the downhillers are speeding. Money has changed it all. Attitudes are extreme and the clamor for glamour and fame has turned the events into traffic jams and environmental disasters. The worst example of this is the twenty-four-hour Moab race that takes place next to a wilderness area. The fragile desert staging area has become like the surface of the moon, and the desert terrain will take 200 years to recover.

This is not to discourage you from racing. There are still local events where the fun outweighs the competition, and the camaraderie is the prime reason for being there. NORBA, the UCI, lawyers, insurance companies, and the greedy promoters are trying desperately to wreck the racing scene for the average Joe, but just remember that the smaller the race, the more fun you are going to have racing. If you are going to watch, the DH and the dual slalom at a national or World Cup race are the places to be.

Mountain-Bike Maintenance

aintaining a standard mountain bike without suspension parts is mostly an easy chore, and anyone can learn the drill. But if you own a full-suspension rig with disc brakes, things can get really nasty and require a serious investment in time, energy, and tools. At any rate, the basic chores of keeping the drivetrain running smoothly and dealing with tires, tubes, brake adjustments, and simple repairs are easy.

Invest in your own set of basic tools if you are interested in maintaining your bike on a regular basis. Here is a list of tools that every home mechanic should have. Check at a bike shop for preassembled tool kits or for some of these specialized bicycle tools.

1. Metric wrenches

    a. Open-end type—sizes 17, 16, 15, 14, 10, 9, 8 millimeters

    b. Allen wrenches—sizes 6, 5, 4 millimeters

2. Chain rivet tool

3. Small slothead screwdriver

4. Tire levers

5. Pair of standard pliers

6. Tube patch kit

With a set like this you can do all necessary basic repairs. The more serious among us can add the following to create a small shop suitable for replacing parts that wear out or for upgrading components:

1. **Bike repair stand**

2. **Crank puller and crank wrench (Allen and/or bolt type)**

3. **Bottom bracket tools (know which tools apply to your specific bike)**

4. **Spoke wrenches**

5. **Wheel truing stand. (Note: You can kill yourself with a badly trued rim. Learn how to do it correctly by taking a course at a local bike shop or reading one of the many manuals on the subject that are available through your local bike shop or through mail order.)**

6. **Headset remover and press**

7. **Pedal wrench**

If you own a full-suspension bike with disc brakes, you will have to deal with another level of knowledge that should be provided by the manufacturer of each suspension component and disc brake system. Read your manuals, and if you are not adept at this kind of thing, go to a good local bike mechanic for help.

Pivots on most full-suspension bikes will have to be serviced. Some are easy, others require special tools and a press. Know your equipment, but don't try things that will ruin your toys. Always err on the side of a good mechanic.

Keep It Clean

The first rule of bicycle maintenance is "Keep it clean." A dirty bike is an unhealthy bike. Mountain bikes get especially dirty and demand special attention. After a dirty ride, wipe your bike down with a damp cloth. If the dirt or mud is thick, *do not* take your bike to the local carwash for the high-pressure hose. A dousing like this could remove the grease from your bearings and freeze up the internal parts. If you have to use a hose, avoid spraying directly on the areas where bearings are located, and use a very low-pressure stream of water. Chains should be periodically removed and cleaned in a solvent. (See "Chain Removal and Repair" on page 68 to remove and replace chain.) Relubricate your chain with a Teflon- or silicone-based lubricant. Be sure to wipe off excess lubricant.

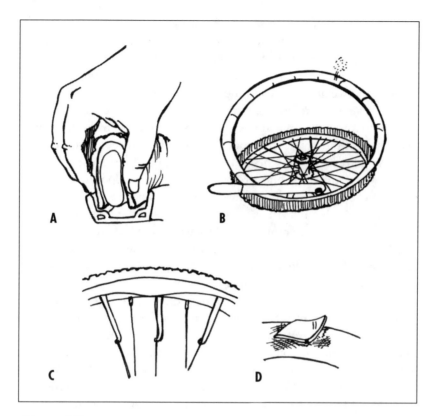

Figure 22
....

Fixing a flat tire
- A) Pinch tire from the side to remove the tire
- B) Pump tire up to find leak
- C) Fix tire using tire wrenches
- D) Patch tire

Fixing a Flat

Some people pay bike shops to do this basic repair. However, there isn't always a bike shop located just around the bend. Part of mountain biking is the ability to perform in-the-field repairs. Fixing a flat is not that difficult (Figure 22). Mountain-bike racers must replace a tube and be back on the road as quickly as possible, often in less than five minutes.

If you hear that hissing sound on your ride or feel that flop-flop-flop below, stop immediately to avoid damage to your tire or wheel. Damage can occur when the rim hits a hard object like a rock or curb. The tire can become shredded and thus unrepairable as it gets crushed between the rim and the road.

To repair a flat, remove the wheel. Close your brake pads against the rim with one hand and release the straddle cable from the non-fixed side of the brake with your other hand. Now let go of the brakes and remove the wheel. If you have a quick-release–style hub (with a lever that flips outwards), open the lever to loosen the wheel and remove the wheel from your frame. If you have a bolted-style hub (one with lug nuts), use a wrench to loosen the nuts, and remove the wheel. Removing the rear wheel is a little trickier than the front wheel. While standing behind the bicycle, reach down and gently pull the rear derailleur back toward you. Then push the wheel forward and down to clear the chain.

Once the wheel is removed, pull out your tire irons. Push the dished end of the irons between the tire and the rim and pry one side of the tire up and over the rim. Some irons will have a hook on the opposite end so you can hang it on a spoke and keep your hands free while you work with a second iron. Take the second iron and pry the other side of the tire off the rim. If you are unable to remove one side of the tire from the rim with just two levers, you may have to repeat the process with a third tire iron. The wide mountain-bike tire usually comes off quite easily, however.

Pull the tube out of the tire while leaving the valve stem attached to the rim. Grab your bike pump and fill the tube with air until you find the hole. Now replace the tube in the tire to find where the corresponding puncture hole is in the tire. Look for a thorn, a piece of glass, or any other object that might have punctured your tube. Remove it. Run your hand carefully around the inside of the tire, feeling for any other possible puncture-makers.

If it is a small hole, mark it and grab your patch kit. Inside you'll find an abrasive pad, patches, and a tube of glue. Use the abrasive pad to lightly roughen the surface of the tube. This creates a better bond between patch and tube. Apply a thin layer of glue to the area around the hole, making it slightly larger than the patch itself. Allow it to dry for several minutes.

Notice that your patch has a plastic side and a foil side. Peel the foil side off the patch, taking care not to touch the exposed area. Center it over the hole with your fingers. Apply pressure to the center of the patch and work out toward the edges. Use the curved edge of a tire iron to apply pressure to the area. Gently peel back the plastic off the top of the patch, taking care not to peel up the edges of the patch off the tube.

Install the valve stem in the rim, and work the tube back into the tire, working in opposite directions and ending across the wheel from the valve stem. Now put one side of the tire back in the rim. Start at the valve stem again, and use your tire levers to work the tire back onto the rim. You will encounter more resistance as you try to work in the last bit of tire. Be careful not to pinch the tube between your rim and the lever or it might get punctured again. Also, be sure that your valve is straight. A crooked valve might break.

As you pump up the tire, watch the edge of the rim. Make sure your tube is not bubbling out from between tire and rim. If this happens, immediately deflate the tire at the valve, gently tuck the tube inside the tire, and reinflate.

Put your wheel back on. Make sure that your wheel is properly secured on the bike with the quick-release or axle nuts. Don't forget to refasten and check your brakes.

Patching a tire is an inexpensive way to fix a flat. But patches can develop slow leaks that could take you by surprise when you are too far from home. I usually just buy another tube whenever I develop a flat. It feels secure knowing that you won't have to pump up your tire every fifteen minutes. Always carry an extra tube and a patch kit whenever you go for a ride.

Truing Your Wheel

When your wheel wobbles or bumps against your brake pads while you're riding, chances are you need to have your wheel trued. Wheel truing is a technique that tightens or loosens spokes to make the wheel round and true. To determine if your wheel needs truing, hold a pencil about ⅛ inch from the rim and spin it. If the pencil touches the rim, or if you squeeze your spokes two at a time and find they feel loose or spongy, you probably should have your wheel trued. This is a technique beyond the scope of this book. If you really think your wheel needs truing, see your local bike mechanic.

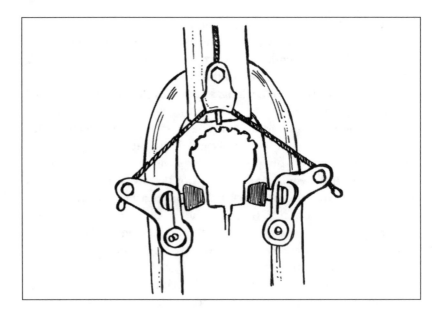

Figure 23

Proper brake-pad alignment

Adjusting Brakes

Brakes are important. They will save your life. You should know
how to adjust them at home and on a ride. Your brakes need attention when you notice one or more of the following:

a) They make an awful squealing noise.

b) Nothing happens when you apply your brakes.

c) You have a pad rubbing constantly on the rim.

d) Your brake pads are in contact with your tire (instead of the rim).

e) You have frayed cables.

Most modern mountain bikes have either cantilever V-brakes (lin-
ear pull) or discs. If you have discs, you are in for a learning curve
that this book cannot provide. If you have V-brakes, maintenance,
repair, and expenses are easy to handle. The techniques outlined
below are written assuming that older-style cantilever brakes are
your brake design. If you have U-brakes or rollercam brakes, consult

your local bike shop for details on repair or adjustment.

Even if your brakes are not causing any of the problems mentioned above, they still need to be adjusted on occasion. First look at where your brake pads come in contact with the rim. The brake pad should be centered on the rim without rubbing the tire (Figure 23). If it is not centered, take an Allen wrench (5 or 6 millimeters) and insert it in the bolt that holds the pad stud. For old-style cantilever brakes, now take a 10-millimeter open-end wrench and loosen the nut on the opposite side of the bolt. This will allow you to maneuver the pad until it lines up with the rim correctly. While performing this adjustment, you want to make sure that the front of the pad (the side that is toward the front of the bike) contacts the rim before the back of the pad does. This should be approximately $\frac{1}{16}$ to $\frac{1}{8}$ inch from the rim. This prevents the brakes from squealing. If you are adjusting Shimano linear-pull brakes, the pads should not have any toe-in and should be mounted flat to the rim surface.

To tighten the brakes, you want to remove the slack from your brake cables. Before you do this, you must turn the adjusting barrel on your brake lever. Turn the barrel clockwise until you have approximately 4 millimeters of threads showing. This will enable you to fine-tune the brakes once the cable is tightened.

Now, compress the brake pads tightly to the rim (with the help of a friend or by tying the pads in place). Then loosen the cable-binder bolt located at the end of the cable. Pull the cable firmly down with a pair of pliers. Tighten the binder bolt while holding the cable in place.

Now give the brake lever a couple of good solid squeezes and then spin the wheel to be sure that the pads are centered and not rubbing on the rim. If they are too close, turn the adjusting barrel on the brake lever clockwise until you have enough clearance on the rim. If the pads are rubbing on one side or the other, slide your cable carrier to the left or right. Squeeze the lever again and recheck your adjustment. In a pinch, you can use the adjusting barrel to tighten your brakes. But don't rely on this adjustment exclusively. It is best to tighten the cable and use the barrel for fine-tuning.

Adjusting Gears

When you shift your gears, you move a lever that pulls a cable. This cable moves your derailleurs (Figure 24). The derailleur moves

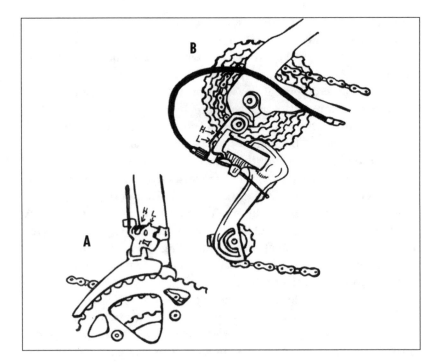

Figure 24

A) Front derailleur
B) Rear derailleur

your chain over the appropriate gear. The chain is prevented from
going too far in either direction by properly adjusted derailleur stops.
Newer bikes have indexed shifting systems with eight or nine speed
cogs on the rear, two or three chain rings on the front, and shifters
that are either thumb and index finger–operated or twist activated.
With the advent of spring-tensioned shifters and reverse-swing
derailleurs, the shifting mechanism can be tensioned either to shift
outward or inward, depending on the specific system. There are a
variety of shifters on the market, and knowing your own specific system will require that you read your service manuals or get some
instruction from the shop where you purchased your bike. Getting
the shifters and derailleurs to operate correctly is simple—even if it
sounds complicated—requiring only common sense and few or no
tools.

An improperly adjusted derailleur causes overshifting (when your chain shifts off the cogs or chain ring or shifts onto adjacent gears out of the indexed sequence), undershifting (when your chain won't shift into the next gear), or automatic shifting (when you haven't even touched the lever). A properly adjusted derailleur hits all your gears quietly, quickly, and precisely as you pedal.

To adjust your derailleur, it helps to have a bike stand to get your bike off the ground. If you don't have access to one, you can hang your bike by its seat and handlebars. First operate the right-hand shifter to shift the chain onto the smallest cog in the rear while cranking the pedal forward. The chain should be on the smallest cog in the rear. If it's gone past and overshifted between the cog and frame, you need to set your outside derailleur stop. This is done by tightening a screw marked "H" (for high gear) on the derailleur. Carefully lift the chain back onto the smallest cog. Then, turn the "H" screw clockwise with a small slothead screwdriver until you meet resistance. Do not overtighten. If you are undershifting and not reaching the small cog, you need to loosen (turn counterclockwise) the "H" screw until the chain engages on the cog.

While you have the chain on the small cog, check your cable tension. Loosen the bolt that holds the cable to the rear derailleur. Grasping the end of the cable with a pair of pliers, gently pull the excess cable slack and retighten the binder bolt.

Now check the low-gear stop on the rear derailleur. While cranking the pedal again, operate the right-hand shifter system so that the chain is shifted to the largest cog in the rear. If your chain shifts between the cog and your spokes, manually lift it back onto the largest cog. Now turn the screw marked "L" (for low) in a clockwise manner until you meet resistance. Do not overtighten. At this point your rear derailleur should be properly adjusted. Check the adjustment by cranking your pedal forward and running through the gears by moving your shift lever forward and back. If the derailleur hesitates or still overshifts or undershifts, readjust the appropriate stop screw.

The indexing of the derailleurs is adjusted by the barrels on the shifters where the cable enters the mechanism and at the rear derailleur where the cable housing meets the derailleur body. Barrel adjustment will move the chain in different directions on different systems. Rapid Fire is standard, Rapid Rise is reversed. SRAM twist shifters also have two different shifting directions. You will have to ask your bike shop just which way to adjust your particular system.

Adjusting the front derailleur is the same as adjusting the rear derailleur; however, there are a couple of things you need to check. With your left hand, release tension on the cable either by twisting outward fully or by pulling the trigger until the cable is completely released. While cranking the pedal forward, look down at your chain. It should be on the smallest chain ring. If it isn't, turn the left-hand screw or the screw marked "L" on your front derailleur counterclockwise. At the same time slowly crank the pedal forward until the chain drops onto the small chain ring. Look directly over the front derailleur and check to make sure that the right-hand edge of the derailleur cage is parallel to the chain rings. If it's not, loosen the bolt that holds the derailleur onto the frame, rotate the derailleur (without allowing it to drop) into a position parallel to the chain ring, and tighten the bolt.

Now take the slack out of the cable. Loosen the cable-binder bolt and grasp the cable with a pair of pliers, gently pulling the cable until snug. Retighten the bolt while holding the cable in place. To set the high-gear stop on the front derailleur, push the left-hand thumb-shifter away from you while cranking the pedal. If the chain falls off the outside of the large chain ring, gently hand-place the chain on the larger chain ring and operate the shifter slightly back so that the front derailleur is centered over the chain. Now take your small slot-head screwdriver and turn the "H" or right-hand screw until you meet resistance. Do not overtighten. Now shift through your front gears to make sure the derailleur is not overshifting or undershifting.

Chain Removal and Repair

Often it is necessary to remove your chain for periodic cleaning or to replace it (Figure 25). Before you mess with the chain, check whether you have a Shimano chain. If you do, you will need to replace the small pin that holds the links together every time you break the chain. Pins can be purchased at your local bike shop for a lot more than you would ever want to pay, but that's Shimano. To remove the chain on a non-Shimano bike, take your chain rivet tool and place your chain within the front guides (farthest from the T-handle). Slowly rotate the T-handle in a clockwise manner, making sure that the pin attached to the handle is pushing directly against the side of

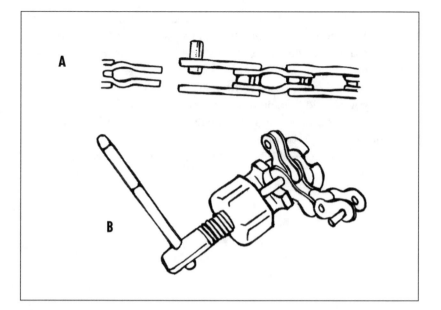

Figure 25
....

A) Chain removal
B) T-handle chain tool

the pin connecting the two chain links in the guides. Without completely removing the chain pin from the links, push it out until the far end is flush with the outside edge of the tool. Turn the T-handle counterclockwise to back it out of the links. Remove the tool from the chain, and gently snap the links apart. One of the links should still contain the pin. If the pin is not in either link, you will need to take the chain to a bike shop.

After you clean the chain, put it back together by reversing the link positions in the chain tool guide. Push the pin back into the links with the T-handle. With the chain back on the bike, slowly crank the pedal backwards and watch the chain run through the rear derailleur cage. It should run smoothly and quietly. If it hops or has stiff links, determine which links are stiff by flexing them with your hands. Grab your chain tool and set the stiff links across the set of guides closest to the T-handle. Turn the T-handle clockwise until it touches the pin in the links and give it approximately one-quarter turn more. *Caution:* Do not turn the T-handle too far. Turn it only enough to loosen the link, not to take it apart. Do this with each stiff link and then recheck that the chain moves smoothly and quietly while cranking the pedal backward. When you're finished, relubricate your chain.

Now you've got the basics. With a little practice and a little patience you should be able to keep your gears and brakes fine-tuned, your tires inflated, and your chain running smoothly. If you have questions or problems with your adjustments and repairs, don't hesitate to see your local bike mechanic and get your bike checked by a pro.

GLOSSARY

Adjusting barrel: Fine-tune tension adjustment on brake lever.

Allen wrench: Hexagonal wrench.

ATB: All-Terrain Bicycle.

Beginner: Racing classification; has never raced before.

Bike stand: Apparatus that lifts bike off the ground to repair wheel.

Binder bolt: Bolt that holds tension on brake cable adjustments.

BMX: Bicycle Motocross; the first bikes to be ridden in the dirt.

Bottom bracket: The bearings and axle of the pedal system.

Butt-bag: A pack carried around the waist. (Also called fanny pack.)

Cable lock: A bike lock consisting of a braided cable; can be cut with bolt cutters.

Cadence: Pedaling rhythm.

Cantilever beam: Rear-suspension system with a single pivoting chain stay.

Cantilever brakes: Brake system that pulls both pads simultaneously.

Chain ring: Cog or gear on pedal side of gear system.

Clean: To complete an observed trials section without a dab.

Clipless pedals: Pedals using a mechanical binding system and a shoe-mounted cleat.

Cog: Gear.

Crank: Stem that attaches pedal to the chain ring.

Cross-bike: *See* Hybrid bike

Cruiser: A low-priced bike that has similar characteristics to a mountain bike.

Dab: To touch your feet to the ground during an observed trials competition.

Derailleur: Mechanism that shifts the chain between gears.

Double track: A dirt road.

Down tube: Tube on bike frame that runs from the fork to the bottom bracket.

Four-bar linkage: A rear-suspension system utilizing a rocker arm and a system of pivots and links.

Freeride: Long-travel, full-suspension bike used for cross-country.

Freestyle: A type of biking where tricks and stunts are performed.

Gear: Cog.

Grip shift: Twist shifters.

Head tube: The short tube connecting the top tube and the down tube, within which the forks and the handlebars are connected.

Hopping: Trials technique where bike is hopped up and over obstacles.

Hybrid bike: A bike that utilitzes both mountain- and road-bike designs.

Hydration pack: A back or fanny pack that carries water in a bladder with a bite valve.

Hydroplane: The ability of the bike to skim over water without touching the ground.

Hyper-glide: Dishes in cogs that allow smoother shifting under load.

IMBA: International Mountain Bike Association; advocacy group for trail access around the world.

Intermediate: Racing classification; has raced five races.

Kamikaze!: A downhill competition held at Mammoth Mountain, California.

Masters: Racing classification; age forty-five and up.

Modified bike: Racing classification for trials: a bike that has been designed for observed trials competition.

Mountain bike: A bike designed for off-road riding.

Mountain touring bike: Mountain bike with modifications for carrying loads.

NORBA: National Off-Road Bicycle Association; oversees mountain-bike racing and access.

Observed trials: Competition where riders negotiate obstacles.

Obstacle: Any rock, boulder, log, stairs, curb, puddle, etc.

Pannier: Bike pack that mounts on the side of the bike.

Racing bike: Mountain bike designed for competition; usually lighter than stock bike.

Rapid fire: Trigger shifting system.

Rapid rise: Trigger shifting system with a reverse-operating rear derailleur.

Rim: Part of wheel that holds tire in place.

Roller cam brake: Brakes that utilize cams to increase tension.

Saddlebag: Pack that hangs under the seat.

Seat tube: Tube on frame that connects seat to bottom bracket.

Section: A complete obstacle in trials.

Shock: Spring and dampener for a rear-suspension bike.

Single speed: Racing classification for one-speed bikes.

Single track: A narrow path or trail.

Skid turn: A turn where the rider skids the rear wheel without stopping.

Slickrock: Geologic formation consisting of smooth sandstone.

Spin: *See* Cadence

Stock bike: Racing classification for trials; normal mountain bike as sold to the public.

Super: Racing classification; top-level amateurs.

Suspension fork: Front suspension system.

Switchback: Where a trail or road that traverses a slope switches directions.

T-handle: Part of chain tool that removes the pin in the master link by rotating it.

Thumbshifter: Old-style shift levers mounted on handlebars.

Tire iron: Long tool with a hook on one end and a shallow dish on the other end for removing the tire from the rim.

Toe clip: Basket or clamp that holds the foot onto the pedal.

Topographic map: Map that shows geographic features as well as roads and trails.

Top tube: Tube that connects seat tube to the head tube.

Trials bike: Bike designed for observed trials competition.

True: Adjust spokes to reduce wobble in the rim of a wheel.

U-Lock: Heavy-duty lock that cannot be cut with bolt cutters.

Unified rear triangle: A rear-suspension system with a pivot in front of the bottom bracket whereby the entire drivetrain is part of the suspended rear unit.

Veteran: Racing classification; ages thirty-five to forty-five.

Wheelie: Technique where front wheel is pulled off the ground.

INDEX

maintenance, 59–70
mountain touring bike, 10

observed trials, 56–57
obstacles, 32–33, 35–42
    urban, 50–51

packs, 21
pads, 23, 35
panniers, 21
price, 5
pumice, 49–50

racing, 53–58
  classifications, 53
  mountain bikes, 8–9
rocks, 39–41

safety equipment, 23, 35
sand, 31–32, 49–50
shoes, 23
single track, 44–46

skidding, 15–16
skills
    advanced, 25–34
    basic, 13–20
slickrock, 48–49
snow, 42
supplies, 21–22
switchbacks, 46

terrain changes, 30–31
tool kit, 22
tools, 59–60
traditional mountain bike, 7–8
trials bikes, 9–10
turning, 14–15

uphill, techniques for riding, 25–28

water, 41–42
weight shifts, 13
wheels, truing, 63